1ST
IN FASHION
x x x x x

CHUCK TAYLOR

SNEAKER SENSATION

REBECCA FELIX

Checkerboard Library

An Imprint of Abdo Publishing
abdopublishing.com

ABDOPUBLISHING.COM

Published by Abdo Publishing, a division of ABDO, PO Box 398166, Minneapolis, Minnesota 55439.
Copyright © 2018 by Abdo Consulting Group, Inc. International copyrights reserved in all countries.
No part of this book may be reproduced in any form without written permission from the publisher.
Checkerboard Library™ is a trademark and logo of Abdo Publishing.

Printed in the United States of America, North Mankato, Minnesota
062017
092017

 THIS BOOK CONTAINS
RECYCLED MATERIALS

Design: Emily O'Malley, Mighty Media, Inc.
Production: Emily O'Malley, Mighty Media, Inc.
Series Editor: Katherine Hengel Frankowski
Cover Photographs: AP Images (left); Shutterstock (right)
Interior Photographs: Alamy, pp. 13, 25; AP Images, p. 7; Courtesy of Abe Aamidor, author of *Chuck Taylor, All Star: The True Story of the Man behind the Most Famous Athletic Shoe in History*, published by Indiana University Press, pp. 11, 21; iStockphoto, pp. 22 (bottom), 23 (middle); Seattle Municipal Archives/Flickr, p. 15; Shutterstock, pp. 5, 19, 23 (top), 23 (bottom), 27; Wikimedia Commons, pp. 9, 17, 22 (top), 22 (middle)

Publisher's Cataloging-in-Publication Data

Names: Felix, Rebecca, author.
Title: Chuck Taylor: sneaker sensation / by Rebecca Felix.
Other titles: Sneaker sensation
Description: Minneapolis, MN : Abdo Publishing, 2018. | Series: First in fashion | Includes bibliographical references and index.
Identifiers: LCCN 2016962492 | ISBN 9781532110788 (lib. bdg.) | ISBN 9781680788631 (ebook)
Subjects: LCSH: Taylor, Chuck, 1901-1969--Juvenile literature. | Fashion designer--United States--Biography--Juvenile literature. | Sneakers--United States--Biography--Juvenile literature. | Shoe industry--United States--Biography--Juvenile literature.
Classification: DDC 391 [B]--dc23
LC record available at http://lccn.loc.gov/2016962492

CONTENTS

SUPERSTAR SNEAKERS

It's after school on a Friday, and you're skateboarding at the park. Your sneakers' rubber soles grip the flat skateboard deck. Their soft yet **durable** high-tops support your ankles. Your sneakers also look supercool! You are wearing All Stars.

All Stars are often known as Chuck Taylors, or Chucks. They are named after Chuck Taylor, the man who made them famous. Taylor was a salesperson for Converse, the company behind All Stars.

Taylor helped make All Stars popular by bringing them to the basketball court. He did this by talking to coaches across the nation beginning in the 1920s. Taylor was a major basketball player and fan. He convinced many coaches that All Stars were must-have footwear for basketball

FASHION FACTOID

More than 750 million pairs of All Stars have been sold since 1932.

All Stars now come in every color of the rainbow. You can even design your own pair!

players. Soon, players across the country were wearing All Stars.

By the 1950s, All Stars had become popular off the court as well. Musicians, actors, and everyday kids and adults had started wearing Chucks. Today, All Stars are an iconic piece of American fashion. They have remained in style for 100 years!

BASKETBALL STAR

〰〰〰

Charles Hollis Taylor was born on June 24, 1901, in Brown County, Indiana. As a child, he went by Charlie. Young Charlie had an older brother, Howard, and a younger sister, Elsie. His parents were Aurilla and James.

The Taylors lived in Brown County, Indiana. There were no high schools near Brown County. So, when Charlie was old enough, his father sent him to Columbus, Indiana. There, he lived with his uncle George W. Taylor and attended Columbus High School.

In high school, Charlie played basketball for the Columbus Bull Dogs. By his senior year, he was the team captain. Charlie was well-known around Columbus. The town and its local newspapers followed the games closely. Great players like Charlie were local celebrities!

On March 19, 1919, Charlie played in his first professional basketball game. He was just 17 years

Charlie's high school yearbook said he was "good-natured." It also said that he never hit an opponent unless that person "hit him first."

old. He played for three minutes for the Columbus Commercials, a team sponsored by the local **chamber of commerce**. The team's opponents were the Camp Grant Five, a military team made up of soldiers. It was Charlie's first step in a lifelong basketball career.

A GROWING GAME

When Taylor was in high school, basketball was a fairly new sport. But its popularity was growing. Professional teams like the Columbus Commercials were forming across the county. So were industrial league teams.

Industrial league basketball teams were supported by corporations and factories. As America's economy shifted from agriculture to industry, these companies became more common. Many had their own basketball teams! These teams played games against one another. The games served as advertising for the companies.

After Taylor graduated from high school, he moved to Ohio. There, he joined an industrial league team in 1921. The team's name was the Akron Firestone Non-Skids. It was named after Akron, Ohio, tire manufacturer Firestone's non-skid tires.

FASHION FACTOID
Chuck Taylor wore a size 10 shoe.

Taylor then moved to Detroit, Michigan. There, he played for the car manufacturers the Dodge Brothers. Next, he played for T.B. Rayl Company, a sporting goods company. But soon, a Chicago-based company caught Taylor's eye, changing his life forever.

Basketball was invented in 1891 to condition young athletes during cold winter months.

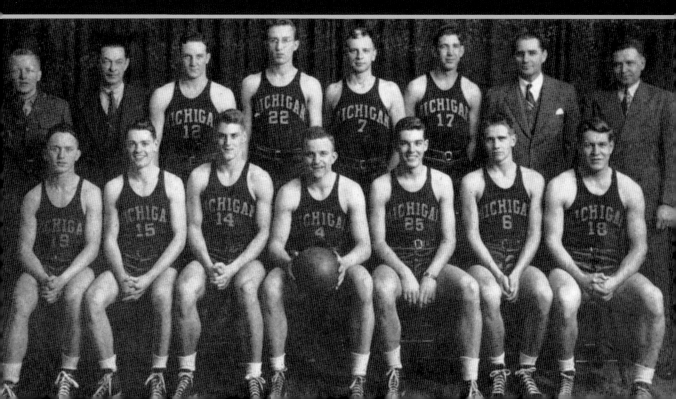

CONVERSE

In 1921, Taylor visited the Converse Rubber Shoe Company offices in Chicago, Illinois. Converse offered Taylor a position as a company salesperson. So, in 1922, Taylor moved to Chicago to begin his career at Converse.

At that time, Converse was an established company. Founded by businessman Marquis Mills Converse in 1908, Converse got its start making rubber **galoshes**. The company had many orders for its waterproof shoes during rainy months. But it needed a dry-weather product.

In 1915, Converse put his employees to work on a new athletic shoe. It had high tops made from double-walled **canvas**. These sturdy tops supported wearers' ankles. Converse's new shoes also had rubber soles and rubber toe bumpers. These features offered improved **traction**.

Converse **debuted** these all-purpose athletic shoes in 1917. They were one of the first pairs of athletic sneakers

Taylor had a lifelong love of basketball.

manufactured in the United States. By 1921, Converse's new shoes were known as All Stars.

Around this same time, Converse began advertising All Stars as basketball shoes. Taylor would help Converse strengthen All Stars' association with the sport. In fact, with Taylor's help, All Stars would become one of the most famous shoes in the United States.

SALES STAR

As a shoe salesperson, Taylor traveled a lot. He met with shoe **retailers** and basketball coaches nationwide. The work suited Taylor. He knew how to listen and build good relationships with his customers.

Taylor cared about All Stars and Converse's financial success. He worked hard to promote the company's brand. He'd visit coaches and describe why All Stars were the best basketball shoes. Eventually, he'd convince the coaches to order All Stars for their teams.

Often, Taylor would even take the deal a step further. He'd visit a nearby retail store and offer them the team

SHOE IMPROVEMENTS

Customers sometimes shared shoe suggestions with Taylor. For example, one customer suggested adding more padding in the ball of the foot for extra cushioning. Taylor brought this suggestion and others to Converse. All together, these ideas improved the shoes.

order he'd just secured. All that store would have to do in exchange was display All Stars in its windows. The process worked. Local stores got business, Converse profited, and All Stars were in shop windows across the country.

Basketball shoes in the 1920s looked very different than shoes worn by players today.

FOR LOVE OF THE GAME

Taylor's sales skills made him successful. So did his reputation as a player. Taylor was well-known in the basketball world. Young athletes and coaches regarded him as a basketball celebrity.

Taylor was also successful because of his basketball knowledge and skills. When he traveled to high schools and colleges, Taylor sometimes **scrimmaged** with players. He'd showed them special tricks. One day, a coach asked Taylor to give his team a few words of encouragement. This would transform Taylor's sales visits forever.

Taylor began putting on basketball clinics as he traveled the country. During each clinic, Taylor shared

MARKETING TRICK

During his clinics, Taylor often challenged a player to stop him from making a basket. When the player failed, Taylor would say the player could have stopped him if he had been wearing All Stars!

his basketball knowledge. He discussed **strategies**, equipment, and uniforms. Soon, his clinics drew hundreds of people. Taylor spread his passion for the sport across the nation, selling All Stars all along the way.

Basketball clinics were popular around the country. They gave players the opportunity to learn and practice new skills.

TRAVEL & TOUGH TIMES

〰〰〰

Taylor spent time on the basketball court during his clinics. He also played for Converse's company basketball team, the All-Stars. Official records only show him as part of the All-Stars during the 1926–1927 season. But many believe he played throughout his time at Converse.

Taylor sold All Stars throughout the late 1920s. During that time, he traveled the country and did not have a permanent address. He slept in hotels and lived on the road. Taylor stored his clothes in a Converse warehouse! It was a busy lifestyle, but Taylor enjoyed his work.

Though Taylor was making sales, Converse was struggling. The company had tried to release a new tire in the 1920s. The tires were not successful, and they cost the company a lot of money. By 1928, Marquis Mills Converse knew he needed to sell his company.

In 1929, Mitchell B. Kaufman, owner of Hodgman Rubber Company, bought Converse. Luckily, many

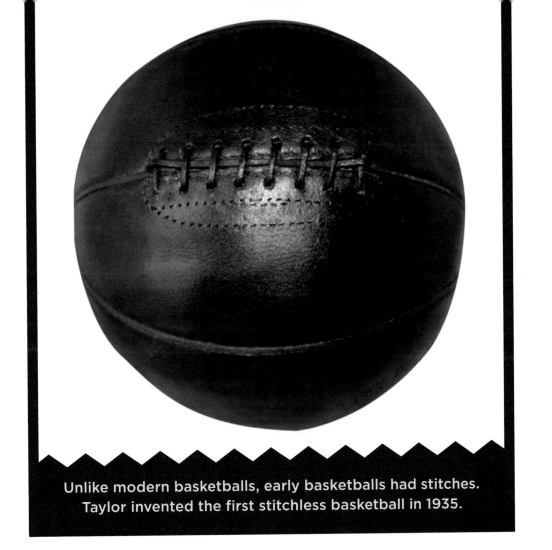

Unlike modern basketballs, early basketballs had stitches. Taylor invented the first stitchless basketball in 1935.

employees kept their jobs, including Taylor. Kaufman sold the company to the Stone family in 1933. They ran Converse for the next 39 years.

ADDING A PATCH

By the 1930s, most people associated All Stars with Taylor. Taylor's friends and customers called him Chuck during those years. So, people began calling All Stars Chuck Taylors, or just Chucks.

In 1932, Converse decided to advertise this connection. The company did so by adding Taylor's signature to the patch on All Stars' high tops. It was the first time in history a celebrity **endorsed** a shoe.

All Stars' popularity as basketball shoes continued throughout the 1930s. In 1936, they became the official shoe of the US Olympic basketball team. Converse created special white **canvas** Chucks for the team. Red and blue stripes lined the shoes' soles.

In 1939, **World War II** began. The United States joined the war in 1941. Taylor began serving in the war two years later. He first served as a troop **recruiter**. Then he worked as a fitness consultant for the government.

At first, the All Star patch was added to give the shoes more ankle support. Now it's an iconic part of the brand!

Later, Taylor coached a US military basketball team, the Air-Tecs, in Ohio. Taylor's players wore All Stars, as did many other military basketball team players. Many soldiers were given All Stars to wear off duty too. Chucks had begun making their way off the court!

RETIREMENT & REBELLION

The war ended in 1945. Afterward, Taylor continued to work for Converse and run clinics. In 1950, he married actor Ruth Adler. The couple bought a home in Los Angeles, California, then divorced five years later. In 1957, Taylor met Lucille Hennessey. Soon after, Lucille divorced her husband to be with Taylor.

Just as Taylor's personal life was changing, so was the **market** for All Stars. During this time, popular actor James Dean was photographed wearing another style of Converse sneakers. This inspired many young people to wear Converse sneakers, including All Stars.

In 1958, Taylor was **inducted** into the Sporting Goods Industry Hall of Fame. He retired from Converse in 1962.

FASHION FACTOID

All Stars were originally available in only black or white **canvas**. Converse started making them in other colors in the 1960s. Basketball teams could then match their shoes to their uniforms.

Taylor (*far right*) was inducted into the Naismith Memorial Basketball Hall of Fame shortly before his death in 1969.

That same year, he married Lucille, and the two moved to Florida. They remained there until Taylor's death on June 23, 1969.

FASHION
TIME MACHINE

PLIMSOLLS, 1870s Invented in the 1870s, plimsolls have rubber soles. The shoes were first used by wealthy Europeans for **croquet** and tennis. They soon became popular with many other people for sports and leisure.

KEDS, 1910s In 1916, Keds became the first rubber-soled shoes **mass-produced** in the United States. They were nicknamed sneakers because they made so little sound when people walked in them.

ALL STARS, 1920s Basketball player and enthusiast Chuck Taylor helped develop Converse All Stars in the 1920s. The shoes are still popular around the world.

ADIDAS, 1960s–1970s Athletes have worn Adidas shoes since the 1920s. Thanks to US tennis player Stan Smith's **endorsement**, Adidas became even more popular in the 1960s. The brand's iconic three-stripe design was introduced in 1969.

AIR JORDANS, 1980s In 1984, shoe company Nike and basketball player Michael Jordan created the Air Jordan shoe line. Air Jordans became extremely popular with players and fans. They remain popular today.

YEEZYS, 2010s Rapper Kanye West worked with Adidas to develop Yeezy Boosts in 2015. The modern design of Yeezys combines comfort, performance, and style. Despite a high price tag, the first Yeezys sold out in just ten minutes!

CHUCKS AFTER TAYLOR

Following Taylor's death, All Stars continued to gain popularity among nonathletes. By the 1970s, Chucks were embraced by punk rockers, skateboarders, and other fashion **rebels**. Meanwhile, other shoe companies such as Nike, Puma, and Reebok emerged. They started making athletic sneakers too.

In the 1980s, basketball star Michael Jordan **endorsed** a pair of Nike sneakers. The shoes, called Air Jordans, became wildly popular with basketball fans and players. By the late 1980s, few basketball players were still wearing Chucks on the court.

Converse's association with basketball may have faded. But sales remained high. This is because Chucks got a major popularity boost from a new style of music and fashion.

In the 1980s and 1990s, grunge bands such as Pearl Jam and Nirvana emerged. The grunge musicians favored

The band Nirvana was hugely popular and helped pioneer the grunge style of the 1990s.

casual, untidy clothing, including worn-out Chucks. The more grunge musicians wore dirty old Chucks, the more their fans did too.

ALL-STAR AMERICANA

All Stars remained popular throughout the 1990s. By the end of 1997, Converse had sold 550 million pairs. People of all ages worldwide were wearing the shoes. They had become icons of American fashion.

Today, All Stars have been worn by everyone from former US First Lady Michelle Obama to cartoon character Dennis the Menace. Basketball players still lace up these classic shoes too. But it's usually off the court.

Modern All Stars now come in many colors and materials. This includes neon colors, the US flag pattern, lace, camouflage, and more. Converse has also partnered with artists, bands, films, and other organizations to make themed Chucks. These included Marvel Comics Chucks, Nintendo Chucks, and even Chucks related to the TV show *The Simpsons*!

In 2003, Nike bought Converse. Nike decided to uphold the Converse brand, given its popularity. Today, the All Stars that Chuck Taylor helped make famous are still worn around the world. And Taylor's signature is still present on every pair of Chucks made today.

Converse shoes and clothing are sold in more than 160 countries!

TIMELINE

1901

Charles Hollis Taylor is born on June 24.

1908

Marquis Mills Converse founds the Converse Rubber Shoe Company.

1917

Converse debuts the first All Star sneakers.

1921

Taylor is hired by Converse as a shoe salesperson.

1920s

Taylor travels the country selling All Stars. He puts on basketball clinics, teaching players and coaches about the sport.

1932

Converse adds Taylor's signature to All Stars.

1950s

All Stars become popular off the basketball court. Musicians, actors, and other people begin wearing them casually.

1969

Taylor dies on June 23.

2003

Nike buys Converse.

GLOSSARY

canvas—a firm, closely woven cloth usually made of linen, hemp, or cotton. It is used to make clothing, tents, and sails.

chamber of commerce—a group that promotes and protects the interests of local businesses in a particular area.

croquet—an outdoor game in which players use mallets to try to hit wooden balls through hoops.

debut—a first appearance.

durable—able to exist for a long time without weakening.

endorse—to publicly recommend a product or service in exchange for money. The act of endorsing something is called an endorsement.

galoshes—a type of waterproof shoe that is useful in snow and slush.

induct—to admit as a member.

market—an opportunity for selling.

mass-produce—to create in large quantities all at once, usually using mechanical processes.

rebel—a person who resists or disobeys authority. The act of rebelling is called a rebellion.

recruiter—a person who tries to get someone to join a group.

retail—related to the selling goods directly to customers. Businesses who sell goods directly to customers are called retailers.

scrimmage—to practice play or a practice game.

strategy—a careful plan or method.

traction—friction between a body and the surface on which it moves. Traction enables the body to move without slipping.

World War II—from 1939 to 1945, fought in Europe, Asia, and Africa. Great Britain, France, the United States, the Soviet Union, and their allies were on one side. Germany, Italy, Japan, and their allies were on the other side.

WEBSITES

To learn more about First in Fashion, visit **abdobooklinks.com**.
These links are routinely monitored and updated to provide
the most current information available.

INDEX